Paris is always a good idea.

Audrey Hepburn

Travel Plan

Date	Departure Time	Departure Airport	Arrival Time	Arrival Airport	Flight No.

Packing List

- ☐ passport
- ☐ boarding passes
- ☐ wallet / purse
- ☐ medication
- ☐ continental Europe travel adapter
- ☐ phone & charger
- ☐ camera & charger
- ☐ memory cards
- ☐ headphones
- ☐ liquids bag
- ☐ deodorant
- ☐ shampoo & conditioner
- ☐ shower gel
- ☐ sunscreen
- ☐ antibacterial wipes
- ☐ sunglasses
- ☐ travel towel
- ☐ socks
- ☐ underwear
- ☐ sleepwear
- ☐ outfits for _ days
- ☐ rain jacket
- ☐ umbrella
- ☐ luggage locks
- ☐ wine bottle opener

Must See Checklist

Monuments and Gardens

- ☐ The Eiffel Tower
- ☐ Notre Dame Cathedral
- ☐ Arc de Triomphe
- ☐ Champs-Élisées
- ☐ The River Seine
- ☐ Jardin des Tuileries
- ☐ Sacre Coeur Cathedral (Montmartre)
- ☐ La Défense

Museums

- ☐ The Louvre
- ☐ Musée d'Orsay
- ☐ L'Orangerie
- ☐ Rodin Museum
- ☐ Centre Pompidou

Extras

- ☐ The Catacombs
- ☐ The Galeries Lafayette

Paris Arrondisements

Paris is a place in which we can forget ourselves, reinvent, expunge the dead weight of our past.

Michael Simkins

An artist has no home in Europe except in Paris.

Friedrich Nietzsche

61

A walk about Paris will provide lessons in history, beauty, and in the point of life.

Thomas Jefferson

You can't escape the past in Paris, and yet what's so wonderful about it is that the past and present intermingle so intangibly that it doesn't seem to burden.

Allen Ginsberg

When spring
comes to Paris the
humblest mortal alive
must feel that he
dwells in paradise.

Henry Miller

We'll always have Paris.

Howard Koch

Printed in Great Britain
by Amazon

33801214R00069